INTERMEDIATE
SIGN LANGUAGE

INTERMEDIATE SIGN LANGUAGE

Louie J. Fant, Jr.

Joyce Media, Inc. • Northridge, California

Photographer: John Joyce
Design: Darlene Heusser
Editorial: J. A. Belcher

Library of Congress Card Number: 80-82631
ISBN 0-917002-54-7

CONTENTS

To Louis and Lillian Beard,
who showed me the way
and inspired me to follow it.

This book is the second in a series designed to provide continuity in the study of Ameslan. The first book, *Sign Language,* is the beginning text and introduces the student to the structure of Ameslan. This book builds upon that structure and attempts to help the student become more proficient in Ameslan.

This book contains approximately three hundred seventy new signs. These coupled with the more than three hundred forty in *Sign Language* give the student more than seven hundred signs.

AMESLAN TRANSCRIPTION SYMBOLS AND ABBREVIATIONS

Capitalized Type   Names or labels of signs are capitalized when printed or typed. (UNDERSTAND, SEE, LOVE).

Underlined Words   Names or labels of signs may be handwritten then underlined. (<u>understand</u> , <u>see</u>, <u>love</u>).

Expression Superscripts   Superscripts above an overline indicating which facial expression to use. These expression superscripts must never be written as if they are grammatical punctuation (UNDERSTAND?) They should be written as follows:

$\overline{\text{UNDERSTAND}}^{?}$# for a questioning expression.

$\overline{\text{UNDERSTAND}}^{!}$# for stress or emphasis.

$\overline{\text{ME UNDERSTAND}}^{\text{neg.}}$# for negation. Signer shakes head negatively while making that sign.

$\overline{\text{RAIN}}^{\text{if}}$// for a "maybe" expression. Signer tilts head forward slightly and raises eyebrows.

Numeral Superscripts   Superscripts which show how many times the sign is to be repeated. WEEK^3 is WEEK signed three times to indicate "weekly."

The end of a statement, analogous to a period in English.

//   A pause, analogous to a comma in English.

⌒   Joins two signs together to form a compound sign. Compound signs flow together almost as if they were one sign. "Good morning" is transcribed GOOD͡MORNING.

≡   Signifies that two signs are executed simultaneously. The left hand does one sign while the right hand does the other. For example:

$$\text{LH:}\overline{\text{YOU}}^{?} \equiv \text{RH:}\overline{\text{UNDERSTAND}}^{?}\text{\#} \text{ or } \text{LH:}\overline{\text{YOU}}^{?} \equiv \overline{\text{UNDERSTAND}}^{?}\text{\#}$$

(. . .)   Labels enclosed in parentheses may or may not be signed; optional. Explanatory remarks may also be enclosed in parentheses.

" . . . "   Quotation marks enclose gestures or mimed actions.

-   Hyphens connect sign labels requiring more than one English word. (UP-TILL-NOW or *up-till-now*). Note that the entire label has a continuous underline.

RH: Right hand signs this.

LH: Left hand signs this.

BH: Both hands sign. For example the FINISH sign may be done with one or both hands. If only one hand is used, it is written, FINISH. If both hands are used it is written, BH: FINISH.

Fingerspelling   Words shown as hyphenated letters (C-L-U-B) are to be fingerspelled.

FF   Face front.

FL   Face left; shows body shift.

FR   Face right; shows body shift.

S   The Signer.

W   The Watcher or Watchers.

-L   Movement is toward the left.

-R Movement is toward the right.

-D Movement is downward.

-U Movement is upward.

-S Movement is toward the Signer.

-R-S Movement is from the right toward the Signer.

-S-W Movement is from the Signer toward the Watcher.

-W-S Movement is from the Watcher toward the Signer.

INX- Index finger points in specified direction, i.e. INX-D means point downward.

SL or **(SL)** The imaginary sight line connecting the Signer with the Watcher or Watchers. See Sight Line Diagram.

Picture Reading Each photograph reads from the Watcher's left to right unless directed to do otherwise by an arrow.

SIGHT LINE DIAGRAM

The sight line (SL) always connects the Signer (S) with the Watcher (W) to whom S is signing. This is true even when relating a conversation S had with Y who is not now actually present. First, S establishes Y in the right or left area. Then S faces Y as if S is actually signing to Y. The revised sight line now connects S and Y. The original W becomes an observer of the conversation between S and Y.

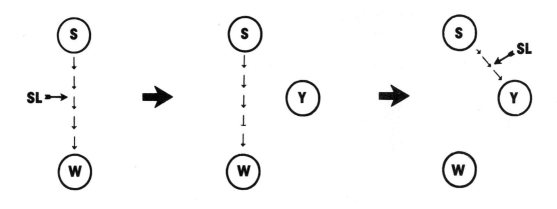

RD　　Area to right and downward of Signer.

RU　　Area to right and upward of Signer.

LD　　Area to left and downward of Signer.

LU　　Area to left and upward of Signer.

U

RU

LU

RD

LD

Lesson
TALK MUCH

There are several signs that have to do with one kind of talking or another, in various kinds of settings. In *Sign Language* you learned three such signs: SPEAK, TELL, and EXPLAIN. Now here are some more signs to help you talk better about talking.

To talk; talk. This sign stresses putting ideas into signs/words, expressing ideas through signs/speech. TALK differs from SPEAK in that it emphasizes the act of uttering words, while SPEAK emphasizes the vocalization of sounds. SPEAK rarely refers to signs or signing, only to speaking vocally, while TALK may refer to vocal speech or signing. Examples:

> INX-R SPEAK GOOD# "He speaks well," meaning he speaks clearly, pronounces well, etc.
> INX-R TALK INTERESTING# "He speaks interestingly," meaning that what he has to say is interesting.
> INX-R SPEAK WHAT-SHRUG# INX-R TALK WHAT-SHRUG# "What's he saying?" "What's he talking about?"
> In this example, the two signs are identical in meaning, so either may be used. If the person being referred to is signing, however, the sentence using TALK would be the one more commonly used.

TALK

To lecture; a talk, a speech, a lecture.

INX-R LECTURE GOOD# "He gave a good talk," or "He speaks well." The "speaks well" has nothing to do with his voice, but with how good a talk he gives.

LECTURE

To preach, to deliver a sermon. When BH are used with the LH turned toward the signer, and moving in the same way as the RH, the meaning is comparable to the English expression, "Practice what you preach!"

PREACH

To discuss, to debate, to talk over.

HAVE ONLY DISCUSS WITH YOU# "I've got something to discuss with you." "I have something to talk over with you."

DISCUSS

To converse with, to communicate, to talk to, to talk with. CONVERSE always implies at least two people engaged in talking to each other.

CONVERSE WANT# "I want to talk to you." There is no need to sign TO YOU.

CONVERSE

CHAT

To chat, to carry on a conversation. This sign usually refers to a very warm conversation with a good friend.

WE-2-R CHAT HOUR[2]# "We talked for hours."

SIGN-CHAT

To chat, or carry on a conversation in signs. This sign has the same feeling about it as does CHAT, except that the talking is done in signs.

To talk in signs. This sign has the same meaning as TALK, with the added aspect that the talking is done in signs. Sometimes it can have the same meaning as SIGN-CHAT.

SIGN-TALK

To gab, to talk excessively. The talking can be vocal or signed.

GAB

To gossip, to spread rumors, to talk about someone.

GOSSIP

This is a variation of the CONVERSE sign. It has the feeling of **there's talk going around.** It may also mean **rumor.**

TALK-AROUND

To argue, to quarrel, to bicker, to fight
(not physically, but verbally, with words
or signs).

ARGUE

To tattle, to tell on someone, to tell a
secret, to inform on, to blab, to squeal
on, to spill the beans.

TATTLE

To tell a story, to relate a story; a story, a tale.

STORY

ADDITIONAL VOCABULARY

Cheap, inexpensive, economical; inferior, shabby, second-rate.

CHEAP

One movement: **almost, nearly, just about.**
Two movements: **easy, facile, effortless;
simple.**

ALMOST; EASY

Excessive, too much, overdone. EXCESS usually follows a verb sign (YOU EAT EXCESS# "You eat too much."), but often comes before an adjective or adverb (YOU CAR EXCESS RAPID# "You drive too fast.").

EXCESS

France; French.

FRANCE

IDIOM WORK

The EASY sign may also refer to personal or moral characteristics.

THINK EASY ME̅# "Do you think I'm a pushover?" "What do you take me for, a dunce?"

WOMAN INX-R EASY# "She's a woman of loose morals." (One can think of a number of expressions that could be used here, but propriety prohibits printing them here.)

EXERCISE

Practice these until you can sign them smoothly and without hesitation.

1. CONVERSE-R F̅I̅N̅I̅S̅H̅# "Did you speak to him?"

2. TALK EXCESS YOU# "You talk too much."

3. DISCUSS PROCEED# "Go ahead, let's talk about it."

4. TELL-R ME ONLY// TELL-S-W OPPOSITE# "He says one thing to me and the opposite to you."

5. TALK CHEAP INX-R# "He's all talk." "Talk's cheap with him." "He talks shabbily about everything."

6. WE-2-R CHAT# WE-2-R SIGN-CHAT# "We had a nice little talk."

7. TATTLE WHO# "Who told on me?"

8. GAB WOW INX-R# "He's a regular motor-mouth."

9. SIGN-TALK HOUR²# "He signed away for hours."

10. LECTURE $\overline{\text{GO-TO-R}}^{?}$ YOU# "Did you go to the talk?"

11. FRANCE $\overline{\text{TALK YOU}}^{?}$# "Do you speak French?"

12. TATTLE EASY YOU# "You can't keep a secret."

Lesson

IDEA

This lesson focuses on how Ameslan deals with statements which in English involve the use of "if." Such statements are called conditional statements, e.g. "If you go, I'll stay here." Ameslan does not use an "if" sign to introduce conditional statements, but rather uses nonmanual cues such as head, shoulder, eyebrow and lip movements, and even eyeblinks.

Linguistic studies done in this area reveal that the nonmanual components of Ameslan are quite complex, and that each signer seems to use the components in different ways, so we cannot yet set down precise rules governing their uses. With regard to conditional statements, we cannot yet say exactly which components to use, nor precisely how to use them. (For an excellent description of nonmanual components in Ameslan, see the chapter by Baker and Padden in *Understanding Language Through Sign Language Research,* edited by Patricia Stiple, Academic Press, Inc., 1978.)

We can, however, describe how a couple of nonmanual components are used in making conditional statements. The head, for example, usually tilts slightly to the side or forward. The eyebrows usually lift. This type of nonmanual behavior is marked in this book with an "if" written above the sign or signs which should be accompanied by the "conditional nonmanual components." For example:

IDEA// $\overline{\text{YOU GO-R}}^{\text{if}}$// ME STAY#, "If you go, I'll stay here."
As you sign, YOU GO-R, you must use at least a head movement and a lifting of the eyebrows. The nonmanual components are necessary to make the signing clear.

To have an idea; to imagine, to suppose; idea, concept. This sign is also used to mark certain conditional statements, for example:

IDEA// $\overline{\text{YOU GO-R}}^{\text{if}}$// ME STAY# "If you go, I'll stay here."

IDEA

Suppose, if, for instance. This sign is used almost exclusively to introduce conditional statements. It may be substituted for the IDEA sign in such instances. For example:

Instead of, IDEA// $\overline{\text{YOU GO-R}}^{\text{if}}$// ME STAY#

you may sign, SUPPOSE// $\overline{\text{YOU GO-R}}^{\text{if}}$// ME STAY#.

SUPPOSE

To imagine, to pretend, to make be-lieve. This sign never means "to have an idea," or simply, "idea," and is never used to mark a conditional statement. It refers to a more **fanciful, day-dreaming, creative kind of imagining.**

IMAGINE

To imagine, to pretend, to make be-lieve, to day-dream. The kind of imagining referred to here is the same as in IMAGINE, but it is more intense, more concentrated.

This sign may also be used to talk about someone being slightly **paranoid,** imagining things that are not true. The nonmanual components, of course, would be quite different.

IMAGINATION

Money, cash.

MONEY

Rich, wealthy. This is a compound sign of MONEY and a sign that means "a pile," or "piled up." The two signs have become so compressed that they now appear as one sign.

RICH

Other expressions that use IDEA to express a conditional statement are:

IDEA// RAIN// ME GO-R# "If it rains, I'm not going." *(if over RAIN; neg. over GO-R)*
IDEA// ME RICH . . . # "If I were rich. . . ." The "if" facial expression is not always used.
IDEA// YOU RICH// DO WHAT-SHRUG# "Suppose you were rich, what would you do?"
IDEA// ME TELL ME RICH// FEEL HOW YOU# "What if I told you that I was rich, how would you feel?"

There are conditional statements which use signs other than IDEA. For example:

SEEM RAIN MAYBE# "It looks as if it might rain."
INX-R FACE SICK SEEM# "He looks as if he is sick." "He seems sick."

The JUDGE sign is often misused by hearing students to express the idea of "if" in conditional statements. This probably happens because the JUDGE sign is used in poetry, songs, lectures, sermons, etc. It seldom occurs in everyday conditional statements. Even in heightened, dramatic, lyrical situations, the IDEA sign is usually better than the JUDGE sign.

One may, of course, always use the fingerspelled sign I-F. Deaf people do it, and the fingerspelling occurs so rapidly that the two letters almost form a sign in themselves. This sign, however, is usually done to mock a person who is forever saying, "If only . . ." When making reference to this type person, or speaking directly to this type person, the signer fingerspells I-F three or four times very rapidly with a sarcastic expression on the face.

There are conditional expressions in Ameslan when no "if" sign is used. For example:

GO-R DON'T-WANT// STAY# "If you don't want to go, then stay here." *(if over DON'T-WANT)*
SICK// GO-R HOME# "Go home if you're sick." *(if over SICK)*
BOOK DON'T-LIKE// READ# "Don't read the book if you don't like it." *(if over DON'T-LIKE; neg. over READ)*

Sometimes in statements of conditions that involve some sort of agreement between two people, the UNDERSTAND sign will be used. For example:

YOU GO-R CAN// UNDERSTAND// ROOM CLEAN FIRST FINISH# "You can go if you clean your room first." (This could also be signed: ROOM CLEAN FIRST FINISH// GO-R CAN#) *(if over UNDERSTAND; if over FINISH)*

ADDITIONAL VOCABULARY

To admit, to confess; admission, confession. This sign is used for such expressions as, **own up to it, tell the truth, to be honest, plead guilty, get it off one's chest, etc.**

ADMIT

To agree, to agree with, to agree to, to be appropriate; agreement. The AGREE sign is also used in the expression, "That dress suits you," or "The color blue becomes you."

AGREE

To blame; to be at fault.   This sign is multi-directional. The RH should hit a glancing blow to the LH and move toward the one being blamed, or held at fault.

BLAME

Fault.

FAULT

A coat, a jacket, a sweater; to put on a coat.

COAT

To disagree, to disagree with, to take issue with; disagreement. As you can see this is a compound sign of THINK and OPPOSITE.

DISAGREE

To be hard-of-hearing; a hard-of-hear-ing person.

HARD-OF-HEARING

To lend, to make a loan; to borrow; loan. In English we say, "I'll lend you the money," or "You borrow money from me," but never, "I'll borrow you the money." Ameslan says them both with this one sign. If the sign moves from W to S, it means, "I borrow from you," or "you lend to me." The sign should move from the lender toward the borrower. This sign is not used in such English expressions as, "Lend a hand," or "Lend me your ears," or "You're borrowing trouble."

LEND

To lose, to be lost; loss, lost.   This sign refers only to losing persons or objects.

LOSE

To lose; lost.   This sign is used to refer to losing in a contest or competition of some kind. It can also mean **failure.**

LOSE-GAME

To make; to build, to construct; to fix, to repair. This sign may also be used as the word is used in English in such expressions as, INX-R MAKE ME SICK# "He makes me sick."

MAKE

(1) To mean, to have meaning; meaning; (2) to intend; intention, purpose.

MEAN

To have a cold, to catch a cold; a cold; handkerchief.

NOSE-COLD

To telephone, to phone, to call; telephone, phone.

PHONE

To postpone, to put off, to delay; to prolong, to extend; to hold over, to lay aside.

POSTPONE

Some. This sign means a certain amount of, or a certain number of, as in "some books," "some people," etc. It is not used in such expressions as, "someone," "something," "someday," or "sometime." For these latter expressions use the sign ONLY, either alone ("someone," "something"), or with another sign: ONLY DAY, ONLY TIME. If distant future time is meant ("someday when you are grown . . .") the WILL sign is used.

SOME

To use, to make use of, to utilize. Do not use this sign in such expressions as, "I used to . . . ," or "I'm used to. . . ." When referring to something that is used a great deal, the sign begins a little higher and moves down a little lower.

USE

Without.

WITHOUT

IDIOM WORK

DISCUSS $\overline{\text{WHAT-SHRUG}}$# "What have you got to say to that, huh?" "What's left to say?" "What could I say?"

DISCUSS $\overline{\text{CLOSE}}$# "End of discussion!" "Enough talk, it's time for action!" "I have nothing to say!"

EXERCISE

Practice these sentences until you can sign them smoothly and without hesitation.

1. IDEA// $\overset{\text{if}}{\overline{\text{POSTPONE}}}$// SORRY YOU# "If you put it off, you'll be sorry."

2. YOU DO $\overset{\text{if}}{\overline{\text{THAT}}}$// SOME PEOPLE DON'T-LIKE MAYBE# "Some people may not like it if you do that."

3. YOU $\overset{\text{if}}{\overline{\text{NOT-YET}}}$// BLAME-S (the movement is toward the signer) DON'T# "Don't blame me if you're late."

4. $\overset{\text{if}}{\overline{\text{DISAGREE-S-W}}}$// DISCUSS# "Let's talk it over if you don't agree."

5. PHONE $\overset{\text{if}}{\overline{\text{USE}}}$// MEAN HARD-OF-HEARING INX-R# "If he can use the phone it means he's hard-of-hearing."

6. IDEA (with a slight nodding of the head)# "I suppose so."

7. IDEA// INX-R $\overset{\text{if}}{\overline{\text{REFUSE}}}$// "shrug" DO MUST ME SEEM# "If he refuses I guess I'll have to do it."

8. IDEA// INX-R ADMIT $\overset{\text{if}}{\overline{\text{REFUSE}}}$// $\overset{\text{!}}{\overline{\text{TATTLE WILL ME}}}$# "If he refuses to admit it, I'll tell on him!"

9. SEEM LOSE-GAME YOU# "It looks to me as if you've lost."

10. SEEM LOSE YOU# "It looks to me as if you're lost."

11. ME MAKE CAR $\overset{\text{if}}{\overline{\text{UNDERSTAND}}}$// YOU CLEAN HOUSE# "I'll fix the car if you'll clean the house."

12. BOOK $\overset{\text{if}}{\overline{\text{LEND-W-S}}}$// HELP-S-W WILL# "I'll help you if you'll lend me your book."

13. COAT WITHOUT// OUT// NOSE-COLD YOU# (OUT may come before COAT) "You'll catch cold if you go out without a coat."

14. IMAGINATION $\overset{\text{!}}{\overline{\text{USE}}}$# "Use your imagination!"

15. $\overset{\text{!}}{\overline{\text{IDEA}}}$# "I've got an idea!"

Lesson
NOT-YET NOT

In *Sign Language* you were introduced to several signs of negation (NO, NONE, NEVER, NOT, CAN'T, NOT-YET, and NO-MATTER). It would be wise if you reviewed the meanings of these signs before going further in this lesson.

There are three important things to remember about negation in Ameslan.

1. Most signs may be negated by simply shaking the head as you sign them.
2. Signs of negation are generally accompanied by the negative head shake.
3. Signs of negation usually follow that which they negate.

Do not, not. This sign is very much like the NOT sign, but usage favors the latter. The DON'T sign is used mostly to give negative commands.

TELL-R $\overline{\text{DON'T}}$# "Don't tell him!"

The NOT sign is used primarily to deny something. TELL-R $\overline{\text{NOT}}$ ME# "I didn't tell him!"

TRUE $\overline{\text{NOT}}$# "That's not true!"

LOOK-R $\overline{\text{NOT}}$ ME# "I didn't look!"

LOOK-R $\overline{\text{DON'T}}$# "Don't look!"

DON'T

Illegal, not lawful, against the rules, prohibited, not permitted, not allowed. This is a very strong sign of negation and usually means that if the person does something that is forbidden, then there will be punishment. It should, therefore, be used judiciously. If you want someone merely to refrain from doing something, do not use ILLEGAL, use DON'T. If, for example, you do not want a person to eat, you sign, EAT $\overline{\text{DON'T}}$#. If it is against a rule for them to eat, sign EAT $\overline{\text{ILLEGAL}}$#.

ILLEGAL

Don't. This sign is a variation of the DON'T sign. It has the same meaning and is used in the same way except that it is a softer, gentler negative command. Rather than give a strong negative command, you are almost asking a person not to do something.

DON'T-WAVE may also be used to deny something, like NOT, but when it is used this way it is a softer, gentler denial. Often the DON'T sign will be followed by the DON'T-WAVE sign to soften the denial.

DON'T (WAVE)

Nothing, not any, not anything. It is identical in meaning to the NONE sign, but is used differently. One difference is that NOTHING is used more in strong denial, or accusatory type statements.

NOTHING

WE DO NONE# "We didn't do anything much."
WE DO NOTHING# "We didn't do anything!"
INX-R DO NONE# "He isn't doing anything."
INX-R DO NOTHING# "He isn't doing a thing!"

Sometimes both hands are used to make the NOTHING sign for a truly forceful effect.

Another difference between the two signs is that NONE usually refers to concrete objects while NOTHING more often refers to abstract things and actions.

ME TELL-R NONE# "I told no one."
ME TELL-R NOTHING# "I told him nothing."
ME SEE-R NONE# "I saw no one (nothing)."
ME SEE-R NOTHING# "I saw nothing."

Unfair, not fair.

UNFAIR

Insignificant, of no importance, trivial; nothing, not any.

INSIGNIFICANT

Worth, important, value, significant; importance, significance. This is not a sign of negation, but in order to understand the next sign, you need to know this one.

WORTH; IMPORTANT

Worthless, unimportant, of no value, useless; in vain, pointless.

WORTHLESS

To refuse, to decline; refusal. This sign is used to convey the meaning of **won't,** and **wouldn't.**

REFUSE

Vehicle, a parked car; park the car, parking. It may refer, of course, to any type vehicle, not just a car.

VEHICLE-PARK (A classifier)

A card, a check, a piece of wood, etc. The specific meaning depends on the context.

CARD (A classifier)

There is a group of signs called "classifiers" that have precise meaning only within the context of a sentence or situation. The VEHICLE sign, for example, may mean a car, a boat, a motorcycle, etc. The sign may also be moved in various ways to convey meanings, such as, "a car going up a hill," "a boat riding the waves," "a motorcycle falling over," etc.

Another classifier is the FINGER-PERSON sign. It may not only mean a person, but also it may be an object, such as a post, or a tree, or it may even be an animal.

Within the group of classifiers is a sub-group called "size and shape specifiers." The CARD sign is a good example.

Quiet, silent; silence; still, calm; still- ness, calmness.

QUIET

IDIOM WORK

To accept, to comply with, to conform to, to resign oneself to, to go along with, to take one's medicine, to put up with.

ACCEPT $\overline{\text{REFUSE}}$# "I won't go along with it!" "I won't take it!" "I'll not put up with it!" DECIDE INX-R// ACCEPT MUST ME# "I'll have to go along with whatever he de- cides."
ACCEPT[3] INX-R# "He does whatever any- one tells him to do." "He'll take anything." "He'll put up with anything."

ACCEPT

To acquiesce; docile, passive, not aggressive. This sign may also convey the meanings given by ACCEPT.

ACQUIESCE

EXERCISE

Practice signing these sentences until you can sign them smoothly and without hesitation.

1. COFFEE DRINK $\overline{\text{NOT}}^{!}$ ME# "I didn't drink the coffee!"

2. MEAN THAT NOT DON'T-WAVE# "No, no that's not what I mean."

3. EAT HERE DON'T# "Don't eat in here!"

4. VEHICLE-PARK ILLEGAL# "No parking here."

5. SEE-R AGAIN $\overline{\text{NEVER}}^{?}$# "Didn't you ever see her again?" or, "Did you never see her again?"

6. MONEY GIVE-W-S NONE// $\overline{\text{UNFAIR}}^{!}$# "That's not fair, you didn't give me any money!"

7. MOVIE SEE NOT-YET# "I haven't seen the movie yet."

8. GO-R NO-MATTER ME# "I'm going anyway." "It doesn't matter to me if I go or not." "I don't care whether I go."

9. TRY FINISH// WORTHLESS# "I've tried, but it's no use."

10. WRONG NONE# "Nothing's wrong." "Everything is all right."

11. WRONG NOTHING# "Nothing's wrong." "I'm okay."

12. NO-MATTER TRUE# "It really doesn't matter."

13. YESTERDAY TELL-S-W CAN'T# "I couldn't tell you yesterday."

14. $\overline{\text{LIKE}}^{\text{if}}$// $\overline{\text{DON'T-LIKE}}^{\text{if}}$// NO-MATTER// GO-R MUST YOU# "Whether you like it or not, you have to go."

15. TELL-R⌢ ME REFUSE INX-R# "He won't/wouldn't tell me."

Lesson
WEEK³

EVERY-MONDAY DRESS WASH-CLOTHES// WASHING-MACHINE DRY SPIN HAVE ME# EVERY-TUESDAY ME GO-TO-R FRIEND HOME// FEW WE MEETING PLAY DEAL-CARDS// DANCE// CHAT// VARIOUS# EVERY-WEDNESDAY ME GO-TO-R VISIT AUNT// SELF-R LIVE NEAR-R# SELF-R OLD BUT MIND GOOD STILL# EVERY-THURSDAY DEAF GROUP BOWLING// ME PARTICIPATE# EVERY-FRIDAY FRIEND JEW WE-2-R GO-TO-L TEMPLE// RABBI LH:INX-L SIGN CAN# EVERY-SATURDAY (SWEETHEART) GIRL FRIEND WE-2-R OUT-R (RESTAURANT) EAT// FINISH GO-TO-L C-L-U-B// SEN-TENCE MOVIE SEE# EVERY-SUNDAY MORNING ME GO-TO-R CHURCH# ALL-AFTER-NOON COUNTRY CAR TOURING PLEASE#

A thing, things, an object, objects.

THING

Each, every. This sign may be combined with ONE to give "everyone"; with THING to give "everything." If EACH is repeated and moved around, it means **every one** of whatever you are discussing, i.e. **each one, everything, everybody,** etc.

EACH

Monday, on Monday.

MONDAY

Every Monday, every week on Monday, on Mondays. All the signs for the days of the week may be treated this way.

EVERY-MONDAY

One movement: **to wear, to put on clothing, to dress, to get dressed.** Two movements: **any kind of clothing, or even laundry.** Many signs such as DRESS distinguish between the noun form and the verb form by changing the movement in some way.

DRESS

To wash anything made of cloth.

WASH-CLOTHES

To wash anything that would be held in one hand while washing.

WASH-DISH

To wash any kind of large flat surface. It can mean to wash windows, to wash a car, or to erase a blackboard. If the action is horizontal and low in the signing area, it usually means to wash or scrub the floor.

WASH-WALL

To wash hands, to wash up, to get washed.

WASH-HAND

To wash one's face.

WASH-FACE

A washing machine; laundromat.

WASHING-MACHINE

To dry, to dry out; dry, arid; boring, un-interesting, dull.

DRY

To spin, to rotate, to revolve. This sign is like the GOING sign, except that SPIN stays in one place. The hands may move to vertical positions to mean spinning like a top, or the Earth rotating about its axis. In this position, the sign may be moved around. Make the action simulate the spinning of the thing about which you are talking.

SPIN

SPIN (VAR.)

EVERY-MONDAY DRESS WASH-CLOTHES// WASHING-MACHINE DRY SPIN HAVE ME# "Every Monday I do my laundry (wash clothes). I have a washing machine and a dryer."

The first person subject pronoun, "I," is usually dropped in Ameslan because it is manifestly clear that S is talking about what S does.

Ameslan usually places the HAVE sign after the thing you talk about having.

The placement of ME after HAVE is a characteristic of the language. One may sign HAVE before "washing machine and dryer," and then sign ME at the end.

One movement: **to have a meeting, to get together.** Two movements: **meeting, convention, assembly.**

MEETING

Tuesday, on Tuesday.

TUESDAY

Every Tuesday, each Tuesday, etc.

EVERY-TUESDAY

Any kind of play activity, but not to be used for dramatic or theatrical type playing.

PLAY

To act (dramatically, theatrically), to perform; drama, play, act, theatre, program, show.

DRAMA

To play cards, to deal out cards; playing cards.

DEAL-CARDS

To dance; a dance.

DANCE

Various, a variety of things, all kinds of things, different things, etc. Signs for generic concepts such as "fruit," are usually conveyed by first signing two or three fruits, then adding VARIOUS.

VARIOUS

EVERY-TUESDAY ME GO-TO-R FRIEND HOME// FEW WE MEETING PLAY DEAL-CARDS// DANCE// CHAT// VARIOUS# "On Tuesdays I go to my friend's home. Several of us get together and play cards, dance, chat, and so on."

The possessive pronoun in "my friend's home" is often not signed. The VARIOUS sign may also be translated, "that sort of thing," or "those kinds of things."

Wednesday, on Wednesday.

WEDNESDAY

Every Wednesday, each Wednesday, etc.

EVERY-WEDNESDAY

Aunt.

AUNT

Uncle.

UNCLE

To approach, to draw near; near, near-by, close, close to. If BH are moved towards each other (they should never touch) the meaning is usually "near." If the hand nearest S remains stationary, and the other hand moves toward it, it means that something is approaching S. If the hand farthest from S remains stationary and the other moves toward it, it means that S approaches something.

NEAR

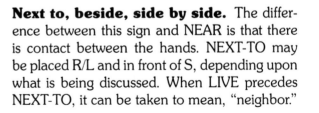

Next to, beside, side by side. The difference between this sign and NEAR is that there is contact between the hands. NEXT-TO may be placed R/L and in front of S, depending upon what is being discussed. When LIVE precedes NEXT-TO, it can be taken to mean, "neighbor."

NEXT-TO

Old, age. If both hands are used, the idea becomes, **ancient, very, very old.**

OLD

Mind, brain, sense.

MIND

Still, yet. This sign conveys the idea of an action or state of being still going on, still happening, not yet ended, continuing.

STILL

EVERY-WEDNESDAY ME GO-TO-R VISIT AUNT// SELF-R LIVE NEAR-R# SELF-R OLD BUT MIND GOOD STILL# "Wednesdays I go to visit my aunt, who lives near me. She is old, but her mind is still good."

In English we say, "her mind is still good," but in Ameslan it is signed, MIND GOOD STILL. The STILL sign belongs to that group of signs that expresses moods, states of being, duration, ability, and difficulty (in this case it is duration), and these signs follow the thing to which they refer. In this sentence, MIND is the subject, GOOD describes its state of being, and STILL indicates that it is presently happening.

Thursday, on Thursday.

THURSDAY

Every Thursday, each Thursday, etc.

EVERY-THURSDAY

To bowl, to go bowling; a bowling ball.

BOWLING

To participate in, to join in, to become involved in.

PARTICIPATE

To quit, to get out of, to withdraw from, to drop out of.

QUIT

EVERY-THURSDAY DEAF GROUP BOWLING// ME PARTICIPATE# "I bowl with a deaf bowling team on Thursdays."

Set up the concrete thing first (a deaf bowling team), then sign the action that pertains to it (join it).

Friday, on Friday.

FRIDAY

Every Friday, each Friday, etc.

EVERY-FRIDAY

Jew, Jewish, Hebrew.

JEW

Temple; synagogue.

TEMPLE

Rabbi.

RABBI

EVERY-FRIDAY FRIEND JEW WE-2-R GO-TO-L TEMPLE// RABBI LH:INX-L SIGN CAN# "A Jewish friend and I go to the temple on Fridays. The Rabbi there knows sign language."

Notice that the action moves to the left this time. There is no particular reason for it other than to remind you that it may go either direction.

The INX sign ought to be made here with a slight arc to it, or it should point into the distance to indicate that the thing to which it refers is not nearby. The larger and slower the arc is made, the greater is the distance.

The CAN sign usually follows the action to which it refers.

Saturday, on Saturday.

SATURDAY

Every Saturday, each Saturday, etc.

EVERY-SATURDAY

Sweetheart, lover. The sign is rather old fashioned, and one does not see it as much as in former years. Perhaps this explains why it is usually done humorously.

SWEETHEART

A restaurant. This is a relatively new sign and there are variants. Check it out with local deaf people.

RESTAURANT

EVERY-SATURDAY (SWEETHEART) GIRL FRIEND WE-2-R OUT-R (RESTAURANT) EAT// FINISH GO-TO-L C-L-U-B// SENTENCE MOVIE SEE# "On Saturdays my girl friend and I ço out to eat. After that, we go to the club to see a captioned film."

Probably S would not use the SWEETHEART sign, but would rather sign GIRL, or GIRL FRIEND. The RESTAURANT sign is optional.

To tour, to take a tour, to go on a trip; to run around from one place to another; sight-seeing. When this sign refers to touring or sight-seeing, the mood that is usually implied is one of leisure, but when it refers to running from one place to another, the mood is one of frantic haste. These "moods" are expressed by specific facial behaviors.

TOURING

Sunday, on Sunday.

SUNDAY

Every Sunday, each Sunday, etc.

EVERY-SUNDAY

**All morning, all morning long, through-
out the morning.**

ALL-MORNING

All afternoon, etc.

ALL-AFTERNOON

All day, etc.

ALL-DAY

All night, etc.

ALL-NIGHT

The rural kind of country, national kind of country. This and the following sign may be used interchangeably.

COUNTRY

The national kind of country, rural kind of country. Both signs for country are used interchangeably.

COUNTRY

EVERY-SUNDAY MORNING ME GO-TO-R CHURCH# ALL-AFTERNOON COUN-TRY CAR TOURING PLEASE# "On Sunday mornings I go to church. In the afternoons, I enjoy driving around the countryside."

In the second sentence here, the order of the signs says first: when (on Sunday mornings); where (in the countryside); how (driving a car); what you did with the car in the countryside (drove, toured around); then finally how you felt about it, the reaction to it (it pleased me).

Think in terms of a movie: first the camera shows us a broad expanse of country, then we see a car driving down a road; the camera comes in for a close up of you driving the car, steering it around curves, and finally we see you smiling, enjoying it.

The CAR sign may be done in ways to show the type driving you are talking about. It may be leisurely and slowly, or it may be tense and rapid. By prolonging the action of the sign, you convey the idea of a long drive.

IDIOM WORK

One movement: **to play baseball; to bat, to go to bat.** Two movements: **a baseball game, a baseball bat.**

BASEBALL

Awful, terrible, dreadful, horrible, etc. This sign, when used idiomatically, may mean: **awesome, astonishing, sensational, terrific, Wow!** When AWFUL is made to convey these idiomatic meanings, it is rarely done from the forehead, but rather done lower down. The hands are often not level with each other. When done this way, AWFUL looks very much like HATE, but the context and facial expression will make it quite clear that S means anything but "hate."

AWFUL

Awful (var.)

BASEBALL $\overline{\text{WOW-AWFUL}}^!$ INX-R# "He is a terror at the plate!" "He's a terrific hitter!" "His power at the plate is awesome!"

WOW-AWFUL

Shape; statue. This sign may be used to indicate any object. Outline the object with your thumbs.

WOMAN SHAPE $\overline{\text{WOW-AWFUL}}$# "Does she have some body!" "She's got a figure that won't quit!"

SHAPE

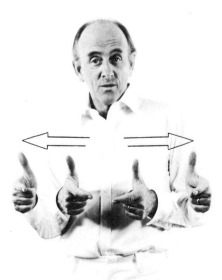

Large, big. When this sign is extended and moved so that the hands make a slight arc, the size indicated gets larger and larger.

HOUSE LARGE (exaggerated) $\overline{\text{WOW-AW-}}$ $\overline{\text{FUL}}$# "The house was a mansion!" "The house was gargantuan!" (Here the AWFUL sign is not translated, because its function is to modify the meaning of the exaggerated LARGE sign.)

LARGE

EXERCISE

Practice signing the seven sentences in the lesson until you can sign them smoothly and without hesitation.

Lesson
WORTH HAPPEN

LONG-AGO AMERICA HAVE SCHOOL FOR DEAF CHILDREN NONE# LH:1≡MAN NAME T-H-O-M-A-S H G-A-L-L-A-U-D-E-T// SIGN GALLAUDET// SCHOOL ESTABLISH WANT BUT// LH:SELF-L TEACH-D DEAF HOW// DON'T-KNOW// SO-SHRUG DECIDE GO-TO-R ENGLAND-R LEARN# ARRIVE-R FINISH FIND SCHOOL INX-R INVITE-S-R ENTER-R REFUSE# GALLAUDET FRUSTRATE GIVE-UP// DECIDE GO-TO-R FRANCE# SUCCESS// SCHOOL INX-R INVITE-S-R ENTER-R# GALLAUDET LEARN² MUCH# GALLAUDET DECIDE GO-TO-L AMERICA MUST// SO-SHRUG GALLAUDET REQUEST-R 1-R TEACH͡ AGENT PLEASE WITH-R-L SCHOOL-L ESTABLISH-L HELP-S-L# THAT-R TEACH͡ AGENT NAME L-A-U-R-E-N-T C-L-E-R-C// SIGN CLERC// SELF-R DEAF# SO-SHRUG// YEAR 18 17 CITY H-A-R-T-F-O-R-D C-O-N-N INX-L// SIGN HARTFORD// GALLAUDET CLERC ESTABLISH FIRST SCHOOL FOR DEAF CHILDREN HERE AMER-ICA CONTINUE UP-TIL-NOW NOW DAY STILL#

VOCABULARY AND TRANSLATION NOTES

America, The United States.

AMERICA

For.

FOR

Here.

HERE

LONG-AGO AMERICA HAVE SCHOOL FOR DEAF CHILDREN HERE NONE# "Long time ago (Many years ago) there was no school for deaf children here in America (The United States)."

The HAVE sign here is translated as "there was." One could translate the idea as, "America had no school."

The numeral "one." This sign sometimes glosses the English, **a,** and **an.**

1 (ONE)

The letter "H." Make it parallel to the sight line, not at a right angle to it.

H

The letter "N."

N

Thomas H. Gallaudet; Gallaudet College.

GALLAUDET

LH:1≡MAN NAME T-H-O-M-A-S H G-A-L-L-A-U-D-E-T// SIGN GALLAUDET// SCHOOL ESTABLISH WANT BUT// LH:SELF-L TEACH-D DEAF HOW// DON'T-KNOW// SO-SHRUG DECIDE GO-TO-R ENGLAND-R LEARN# "A man named Thomas H. Gallaudet, signed 'Gallaudet,' wanted to establish (found) a school, but he did not know how to teach deaf children, so he decided to go to England in order to learn."

The use of the left hand to sign 1, and the right hand simultaneously to sign MAN, is an expedient and efficient way to convey as much information as possible with as little movement as possible.

When fingerspelled letters are used as initials (N.A.D., I.B.M., etc.) the hand is often moved in a circle.

The Ameslan phrase, TEACH-D DEAF HOW// DON'T-KNOW, is an example of the rhetorical question device which is used a great deal in Ameslan. The signer asks a question, then answers it. Interrogatives are seldom used in Ameslan except to ask questions.

The TEACH sign is done slightly downwards to imply the teaching of children.

The GO-TO sign is being directed toward the right here because the man, Gallaudet, was placed on the left. It could have been the other way around, but the important thing is to put him on one side, then "go" to England on the other side of the sight line.

To find, to discover, to uncover, to come across; discovery.

FIND

To invite; to welcome; to hire. This sign is directional and should be made so that it moves from the "invitee" towards the "invitor," or from the "employee," towards the "employer."

INVITE

ARRIVE-R FINISH FIND SCHOOL INX-R INVITE-S-R ENTER-R REFUSE# "When he got there, he found that the schools refused to welcome him in."

Remember that the ARRIVE sign may be translated into the English expression, "get to (a place)." Also, when the ARRIVE sign is made toward the right, it is visually clearer if the LH does the action instead of the RH. If the RH does the action then the left arm is forced to cover the chest area in order to be in the correct position. This "closes up" the signing area in front of the chest more so than if the left arm moves into that area then moves quickly out of it, as it does if the LH is the operant hand.

One of the most common errors learners of Ameslan make is to sign WHEN in statements like the one above ("When he got there, . . ."). The sign WHEN is an interrogative and should be used almost entirely in questions that ask, "When?" One of the functions of the FINISH sign in Ameslan is to indicate that when one event ended, another one began. (For a more complete discussion of the uses of FINISH, see Lesson 7 in *Sign Language*.)

To be frustrated, to be thwarted, to suffer set-backs. If BH are used alternately, it indicates that the frustration lasted over a period of time, or occurred frequently.

FRUSTRATE

To give up, to yield, to surrender, to sacrifice.

GIVE-UP

GALLAUDET FRUSTRATE GIVE-UP// DECIDE GO-TO-R FRANCE# "In frustration, Gallaudet gave up and decided to go to France."

The GO-TO sign moves to the right again. The signer may do this because Gallaudet is "in" England and not America when this sentence is signed. I choose not to go to the left because I want to save that area for "America." Furthermore, going to the right for England, then going to the right again for France conveys a sense of traveling farther and farther from the point of origin, "America," which is on the left.

SUCCESS// SCHOOL INX-R INVITE-S-R ENTER-R# "Finally (At last), a school there welcomed him in."

In this sentence and the one before it, the ENTER sign is used, not the IN sign. The idea is that Gallaudet went into, he entered the school, not just that he was in it.

Long. Used to describe lengths of time. It may be used to refer to books, stories, plays, etc., because the implication is that they take much time to read, tell, or see. It is rarely used to refer to the lengths of concrete objects.

LONG

More, in addition; furthermore.

MORE

To request, to ask for; to pray. When simple asking, or questioning is meant, the QUERY sign is usually preferred.

REQUEST

GALLAUDET LEARN² MUCH# GALLAUDET DECIDE GO-TO-L AMERICA MUST//
SO-SHRUG GALLAUDET REQUEST-R 1-R TEACH AGENT PLEASE WITH-R-L
SCHOOL-L ESTABLISH-L HELP-S-L PLEASE# "Gallaudet learned a great deal. He
decided that he had to return to America, so he asked a teacher if he would please
accompany him back and help set up a school."

The repetition of the LEARN sign implies that he learned a lot, or he worked hard at
learning, or that he spent a lot of time learning. The MUCH sign reinforces this idea.

Note the position of the WANT sign. It belongs to that group of signs that expresses an
emotion, and these signs tend to follow that to which they refer.

Now the GO-TO sign moves to the left, the place reserved for "America." Since this is
the place Gallaudet began from, it is translated as, "go back," or "return."

The PLEASE sign usually follows that to which it refers, but it may come before, then
be copied afterwards.

When the WITH sign is moved as it is here, it means, "to go with," or "to accompany."
Naturally it should move from "France" to "America."

The HELP sign, like the WANT sign tends to follow the thing for which one wants help.
It is marked here "S-L," instead of "R-L," but the meaning is that Clerc is being asked to
help. It is not signed "R-L" simply because "S-L" is shorter, easier, and still clearly understood.

Laurent Clerc.

CLERC

The numeral "17."

17 (SEVENTEEN)

The numeral "18."

18 (EIGHTEEN)

Hartford, Connecticut. In many areas, this is also the sign for **history.**

HARTFORD; HISTORY

THAT-R TEACH AGENT NAME L-A-U-R-E-N-T C-L-E-R-C// SIGN CLERC// SELF-R DEAF# SO-SHRUG// YEAR 18 17 IN CITY H-A-R-T-F-O-R-D C-O-N-N INX-L// SIGN HARTFORD// GALLAUDET CLERC ESTABLISH FIRST SCHOOL FOR DEAF CHILDREN HERE AMERICA CONTINUE UP-TIL-NOW NOW DAY STILL# "That teacher's name was Laurent Clerc, signed 'Clerc,' who was himself deaf. So, in 1817 in Hartford, Connecticut, signed, 'Hartford,' Gallaudet and Clerc founded the first permanent school for deaf children in America that is still in existence today." ("Clerc" is pronounced, "Clere.")

The SELF-R sign is here translated, "himself." It is a little more emphatic than the INX-R sign, and adds the idea of "himself."

English says, "Gallaudet and Clerc," but Ameslan generally does not require the AND sign.

The order of the signs in the second sentence here reflects a very general pattern of Ameslan. First give a date, then a place, then what happened there.

The use of NOW DAY following UP-TIL-NOW creates a more emphatic statement than using the UP-TIL-NOW sign by itself.

IDIOM WORK

The CORRECT sign, when repeated, usually means "regularly." However, when it is used to describe the behavior of a person, it means that the behavior described is very typical of that person.

INX-R LATE ALWAYS CORRECT^2# "He is always late," "To be late is typical of him," "Trust him to be late."

The repeated CORRECT sign might be used also to speak of the inevitability of something.

ME COUNTRY TOURING $\overset{\text{if}}{\overline{\text{WANT}}}$// RAIN// CORRECT^2# "As sure as I want to take a drive in the country, it'll rain." "Just let me take a drive in the country and it's sure to rain."

EXERCISE

Practice signing the story until you can do it smoothly and without hesitation.

Lesson
STORY TRUE

ONE TIME DEAF MAN ENTER-R P-O BUILDING LARGE FOR BUY STAMP# LINE-UP STAND LATER(slowly) STAMP BUY FINISH// WALK OUT-L MEAN// BUT HAPPEN MAGAZINE SELL HAVE INX-R# FINGER-GO-R MAGAZINE BUY WANT# DEAF MAN LH:FIVE-DOLLAR≡GIVE-R(RH only)# MAN LH:TALK-L// DEAF MAN LOOK-R// LIP-READ CAN'T# SEE-R SELF-R $\overline{\underset{!}{BLIND}}$// $\overline{\underset{?}{DO\text{-}DO}}$# BLIND MAN LH:QUERY-L MAGAZINE COST HOW-MANY AND MONEY GIVE-R(RH only) HOW-MANY# DEAF MAN STUN// CONVERSE-R HOW// STUCK# HAPPEN OTHER MAN LH:FINGER-GO-L-S// DEAF MAN EXPLAIN-L TRY (mime: pointing to ears, shaking head, pointing to price on magazine, show inability to speak, etc.)# MAN LH:INX-L≡UNDERSTAND// EXPLAIN-R BLIND MAN FIN-ISH// DIFFICULT MELT#

VOCABULARY AND TRANSLATION NOTES

To build, to construct; a building, a structure.

BUILDING

One movement: **to buy, to purchase.** Two movements: **to go shopping, to buy many things.**

BUY

Postage stamp, postage.

STAMP

ONE TIME DEAF MAN ENTER-R P-O BUILDING LARGE FOR BUY STAMP# "One day (One time; Once) a deaf man went into a large post office building to buy stamps."

The TO sign is rarely used as part of a verb sign (to buy), since its meaning is "toward," or "until." Instead, the FOR sign, which conveys the idea of "for the purpose of," is used with the verb sign, BUY.

To line up, to get in line, to form a line; to walk in a line. This sign may also refer to objects such as cars, chairs, etc. being in a row or lined up.

LINE-UP

A magazine, a journal. This sign may refer to any kind of bound or stapled magazine-like object such as **a newsletter, a bulletin,** etc.

MAGAZINE

One movement: **to sell.** Two movements: **store.** The sign for store varies around the country, so check with local deaf people for the sign they use. The repeated SELL sign may also refer to deaf peddlers who sell the manual-alphabet cards.

SELL

LINE-UP STAND LATER(slowly) STAMP BUY FINISH// WALK OUT-L MEAN// BUT HAPPEN MAGAZINE SELL HAVE INX-R// FINGER-GO-R MAGAZINE BUY WANT#
"He stood in line for awhile, bought the stamps, then meant to walk out, but there happened to be a magazine stand there, so he went over to it because he wanted to buy a magazine."

When the LATER sign is done slowly, it indicates a passage of time that is more than just, "later." One usually translates it as, "after a while," but the length of time will depend upon how slowly the sign is made.

The use of the MEAN sign here shows that the man meant, or intended to walk out.

The rationale for the order of signs in the phrase, MAGAZINE BUY WANT, is that the concrete thing (magazine) comes first, then the action that is related to it (buying) comes next, with the emotional response (wanting) following that to which it relates (buying).

Five dollars, a five dollar bill; fifth.

FIVE-DOLLAR; FIFTH

To lipread, to read lips, to speech-read. This sign is usually used when referring to the oral method, or to schools which use the oral method. Because of this, it is often incorrectly used by learners of Ameslan to mean "speech."

LIPREAD

DEAF MAN LH:FIVE-DOLLAR≡GIVE-R(RH only)# MAN LH:TALK-L// DEAF MAN LOOK-R// LIPREAD CAN'T# "The deaf man handed a five dollar bill to the vendor, who said something to the deaf man. The deaf man looked at him, but couldn't read his lips."

The GIVE sign here is made only with the right hand, and the hand does not open as it normally does for this sign. This becomes a mimetic gesture, as if you handed the bill to the man. A piece of paper, or some object which you would hold until it was taken from you, would cause GIVE to be signed this way.

Although the TALK sign means "he talked," it is here translated as ". . . said something." The TALK sign here must move to the left to show that the vendor is talking to the deaf man, and it is easier and clearer if it is made with the left hand.

The spatialization of the deaf man on the left naturally requires that the LOOK sign be aimed to the right, toward the vendor.

Unable to see; a blind person; blind-ness. This sign may be used figuratively, as in, "He was blind to his own faults."

BLIND

(1) To cost, to charge; the cost, the charge; (2) to penalize, to tax, to fine; penalty, tax, fine.

COST

What do I do now? Now what? What's to be done about it? Hold hands upside down and finger spell "do" rapidly several times.

DO-DO

How many; how much.

HOW-MANY

To be stunned, to be shocked, to be at a loss for words; to faint.

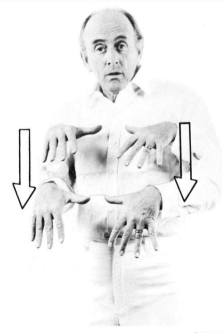

STUN

To be stuck, to be hung up, to be in a fix.

STUCK

SEE-R SELF-R $\overline{\text{BLIND}}^!$// $\overline{\text{DO-DO}}^?$# BLIND MAN LH:QUERY-L MAGAZINE COST HOW-MANY AND MONEY GIVE-R(RH only) HOW-MANY# "The deaf man saw that the man was blind! What was he going to do now? The blind man asked the deaf man how much the magazine cost, and how much money he had given him."

DEAF MAN $\overline{\text{STUN}}^!$// CONVERSE-R HOW// $\overline{\text{STUCK}}^!$# "The deaf man was stunned, he didn't know how he was going to talk to the blind man." A slightly freer translation is: "The deaf man gulped and wondered how the heck he could talk to the blind man."

The STUCK sign is not translated here. Just as one should not try to translate every single word into signs, one should not try to translate each sign into a word.

To explain, to describe, to define; explanation, description, definition. Often when this sign is used, it may best be translated as, **let me tell you what happened.**

EXPLAIN

HAPPEN OTHER MAN LH:FINGER-GO-L-S// DEAF MAN EXPLAIN-L TRY (mime: explaining the problem)# "Just then another man walked up and the deaf man tried to explain to him that he couldn't hear or speak."

The hearing man comes up from the left side and is standing to the left side of the deaf man, so the EXPLAIN sign must be made toward the left side.

Difficult, hard; difficulty; problem. If the hands twist against each other rather than graze each other in an up and down movement, it means **hard times.**

DIFFICULT

To melt, to dissolve; to disappear, to go away; to solve.

MELT

MAN LH:INX-L≡UNDERSTAND// EXPLAIN-R BLIND MAN FINISH// DIFFICULT MELT# "The hearing man understood, explained to the blind man, and then everything was okay."

The two signs DIFFICULT MELT mean that the problem, the difficulty, the situation, was solved, it disappeared.

IDIOM WORK

The FAMOUS sign may be used so that it means much the same thing the repeated CORRECT idiom does.

INX-R LATE[2] FAMOUS# "He's always late." "To be late is his nature." "Trust him to be late." Instead of signing ALWAYS after LATE, just repeat the LATE SIGN.

EXERCISE

Practice signing the story until you can sign it smoothly and without hesitation.

Lesson
DREAM AWFUL

FEW DAY PAST// ME AWAKE STAND-UP BATH SHAVE-FACE DRESS FINISH// GO-TO-R SIT EAT# WIFE QUERY-R-S//

FL:EAT WANT WHAT-SHRUG#

FR:TELL EGG#

FL:COOK HOW#

FR:MIX#

FL:BACON SAUSAGE WANT WHICH#

FR:SAUSAGE#

FL:O-J WANT#

FR:O-K#

FL:TOAST WANT HOW-MANY#

FR:2#

FF:GO-R COOK# COFFEE DRINK PAPER READ// LATER EAT BRING-R-S# WIFE SIT-R(RH only)// TELL-R ME//

FL:FACE TIRED YOU// $\overline{\text{THRILL}}^{?}$#

FR:SLEEP GOOD NOT//DREAM BOTHER-ME[2]#

FL:DREAM WHAT-SHRUG#

FR:REMEMBER CAN'T// MELT(on forehead)#

FL:ME SLEEP//FEEL VIBRATION AWAKE LH:SEE-L// YOU L-E-G "use arms as legs, flail them," "gesticulate wildly with arms"// OGLE-L-D PUZZLED#

FR:THAT// REMEMBER NOW// DREAM WATER WAVE ME SWIM// DIRT NEXT-TO NONE// BOAT NONE// $\overline{\text{LH:SEE-L≡S-H-A-R-K}}$ SHARK// ME SWIM(vigorously) SHARK CHASE// THAT#

FL:THAT// PAST NIGHT T-V MOVIE J-A-W-S LOOK//

FF:EAT FINISH// BRUSH-TEETH FINISH// GONE-R WORK ME#

VOCABULARY AND TRANSLATION NOTES

To bathe, to take a bath. This is another variation of the WASH sign.

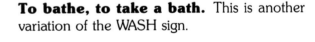

BATH

One movement: **to shave, to get shaved.**
Two movements: **razor.** Although the sign
looks like the old fashioned straight razor, it refers to the modern safety razor as well.

SHAVE-FACE

An electric shaver, electric razor.

ELECTRIC-SHAVER

FEW DAY PAST// ME AWAKE STAND-UP BATH SHAVE-FACE DRESS FINISH// GO-TO-R SIT EAT# "A few days ago, I got out of bed, took a bath, shaved, got dressed, and sat down to eat."

The two signs AWAKE GET-UP are glossed by the English, "got out of bed." The use of GO-TO-R implies that S went from one room to another.

WIFE QUERY-R-S
FL:EAT WANT WHAT-SHRUG# "'What do you want for breakfast?' my wife asked."

The "FL" means to face toward the left, slightly off the SL. Do not turn too far to L/R. One should never turn more than forty-five degrees off the SL.

Facing to the L/R areas is Ameslan's way of showing direct discourse. When facing is done, S assumes the role of the person being quoted.

An egg, eggs.

FR:TELL EGG# "'Eggs,' I answered."

EGG

To cook, prepare a meal; stove; kitchen.

FL:COOK HOW# "'How do you want them?' she asked."

COOK

To mix, to mix up, to blend; to become mixed up, to become confused; confusion, mixed up.

FR:MIX# "'Scrambled,' I said."

In this context, the MIX sign could only mean "scrambled."

MIX

Bacon, a strip of bacon.

BACON

Sausage; hot dog, frankfurter, weiner; bologna.

FL:BACON SAUSAGE WANT WHICH#
"'Do you want bacon or sausage?' she asked."

FR:SAUSAGE#

SAUSAGE

The letter "J."

J

An orange; the color orange. There are different signs for "orange," so check this out with local deaf people.

FL:O-J $\overline{\text{WANT}}^?$# "'Do you want orange juice?' she asked."

One could sign ORANGE instead of O-J. There is no sign for "juice," but in this context just the sign ORANGE would mean "orange juice."

ORANGE

Toast, a piece of toast.

FL:TOAST WANT HOW-MANY# "'How many pieces of toast do you want?' she asked."

Like any other interrogative, HOW-MANY comes at the end of the question.

FR:2# "'Two,' I said."

TOAST

To read, to peruse. This sign may be done several ways. One way is moving the RH from L-R.

READ

To read, to peruse. A second way to sign read is by moving the RH downward.

READ

To read, to peruse. A third way to sign read is to combine the movements of the first and second ways, moving the RH from L-R and downward.

Another variation which means to **read a book leisurely** is to sign BOOK first, then the RH signs LOOK and moves as if it were turning the pages of the book.

READ

FF:GO-R COOK# COFFEE DRINK PAPER READ// LATER EAT BRING-R-S# "She went to the kitchen (went to cook), I drank my coffee and read the paper. After awhile, she brought the food in."

The "FF" tells W that S is no longer playing the role of his wife nor himself, but is now speaking as the narrator. (FF means "face front.")

The order of the signs here illustrates the pattern of putting concrete objects first then following them with the action (COFFEE DRINK, PAPER READ, EAT BRING).

Get used to thinking of the LATER sign as "after awhile."

SIT-R(RH only) This is a way of saying that someone is sitting to S's right, facing toward S. The sign could be made to the L, and could face in various directions. If BH are used, and placed so that the "legs" of the people are facing each other, then it means "sitting face to face."

SIT (POSITIONED)

To be tired, to be weary, to be fatigued, to be worn out; tired, weary, fatigued, worn out.

WIFE SIT-R(RH only)// TELL-R͡ ME//
FL:FACE TIRED YOU// T͡H͡R͡I͡L͡L# "My wife sat down and said, 'You look tired, what's the matter?'"

TIRED

One movement: **To interfere, to interrupt, to block; interference, interruption, blockage;** Two movements: **to bother, to be a nuisance; a bother, a nuisance.** Since BOTHER is multi-directional, hold the hands so that the action moves toward the person or object being "bothered," or "interrupted."

BOTHER

FR:SLEEP GOOD NOT// DREAM BOTHER-ME²# "'I didn't sleep good, a dream kept waking me up (bothering me),' I said."

The repetition of the BOTHER sign here conveys the feeling that the action took place over and over. The manner in which the repetition is done conveys different meanings. Here, for example, it means, "kept bothering me." A slower repetition may mean, "bother continuously." A still slower repetition may mean, "bother occasionally." A very fast repetition may mean, "bother often."

FL:DREAM WHAT-SHRUG# "'What did you dream about?' she asked."

FR:REMEMBER CAN'T// MELT(on forehead)# "'I can't remember,' I said."

The MELT sign placed on the forehead means that something has faded from memory. In this sentence, it is used to reinforce the "forgetting," so it is not necessary to translate it.

Any kind of vibration or shaking. The movement will vary according to the kind of vibration meant.

VIBRATION

To ogle; to glance at; to track with eyes; to eye. This sign is used when S wants to show the movement of the eyes. The meaning will depend upon how the "eyes" move. OGLE-U: to look upwards; OGLE-L-R: to look from the left to the right, to follow something with your eyes. It may mean "glance," showing the direction of the glance.

OGLE

To be puzzled, to be confused; puzzling, quizzical.

PUZZLED

FL:ME SLEEP// FEEL VIBRATION AWAKE LH:SEE-L// YOU L-E-G "use arms as legs, flail them" "gesticulate wildly with arms"// OGLE-L-D PUZZLED# "My wife said, 'I was sleeping and I felt the bed shaking, and it woke me up. I looked over at you and your legs and arms were flying and kicking all around. I couldn't figure out what was happening.'"

Here S plays the role of his wife describing the scene she saw.

There is no sign for "leg" in Ameslan. You may point to them, but it is more common to fingerspell. Often, as is the case here, the fingerspelled word is followed by the arms showing what the legs did. Then follow this by letting the arms show what they did.

The OGLE sign is used when S wishes to accentuate the action of the eyes.

This sentence is a good example of how complex Ameslan can be with regard to roleplaying. First, S plays the role of his wife awakening from her sleep. Then S plays the role of his wife re-enacting what S was doing in his sleep. Then S plays the role of his wife again being puzzled.

Water.

WATER

A wave of water. When this sign is combined with WATER, it may mean "ocean," or "sea." By varying the movement of the sign, you may show stormy waves, ordinary waves, or hardly any waves at all. Other variations may mean "river," "rapids," "waterfall," etc.

WAVE

To swim, swimming; pool, any place for swimming.

SWIM

Dirt, soil; land.

DIRT

Boat, ship.

BOAT

A shark. This is a rather new sign, so when it is introduced, the word, "shark" should be fingerspelled first.

SHARK

FR:THAT// REMEMBER NOW// DREAM WATER WAVE ME SWIM// DIRT NEXT-TO NONE// BOAT NONE// L̄H̄:SEE-L≡S-H-A-R-K SHARK// ME SWIM(vigorously) SHARK CHASE// THAT# "'Oh yeah, now I remember,' I said, 'I dreamed I was swimming in the ocean and there was no land nor boat near by. Suddenly, I saw this shark, and I started swimming like crazy, and the shark chased me! That's what it was.'"

Using both hands for L̄H̄:SEE-L≡S-H-A-R-K gives dramatic emphasis to the statement.
The THAT sign at the end is done in a reflective way, making it different in meaning from the THAT sign which was done at the beginning. The first one is more of a mild surprise, while the second is more like smiling to oneself.

FL:THAT// PAST NIGHT T-V MOVIE J-A-W-S LOOK// THAT͡ YOU# " 'Oh I know,' she said, 'you watched *Jaws* last night on TV, that's what it was.' "

Here the THAT sign shows a flash of understanding, as if S's wife just made the connection between the dream and the movie.

The THAT YOU signs at the end of the statement are usually done so rapidly that they appear to be one sign. It is actually a compound of the two signs. Usually it means, "that's the one," but here it is translated as "that's what it was." It could have been glossed as well by such expressions as, "that's what got to you," "that's why you did what you did," etc.

To brush one's teeth; toothbrush.

BRUSH-TEETH

To go, to be gone, to be absent. This is another sign for "going." The emphasis of this sign is on not being here, being gone, being away from here.

FF:EAT FINISH// BRUSH-TEETH FINISH// GONE-R WORK ME# "After I ate, I brushed my teeth, then I went to work."

GONE

IDIOM WORK

As we learned in the lesson, the MELT sign, when placed on the forehead meant that the memory of something faded away, disappeared. If S had been talking about a headache, then the MELT sign would have meant that the headache had gone away.

If S had been talking about being sick, and placed the MELT sign near his stomach, it would have meant that the sickness or nausea had gone away.

If S describes a pain in his shoulder, then puts the melt sign on the shoulder, it signifies that the pain there went away.

If S describes some sort of disturbance such as a riot, then uses the MELT sign, it means that everything quieted down.

If S talks about a problem, then uses the MELT sign, it means that everything settled down and the problem was solved.

EXERCISE

Practice signing the story until you can do it smoothly and without hesitation.

Lesson
MUSIC QUOTE STAR
SPECKLE FLAG

There exists in Ameslan little if any of what could be defined by hearing people as singing. Almost all that does exist is in the nature of translated work. That is to say, deaf people do not generally compose songs, and there are few (I know of none) songs originally composed in Ameslan. The reason is of course that most deaf people do not hear music, and thus its beauty is of little meaning to them. They can feel the rhythmical beat, and do enjoy this to some extent. Deaf people like to dance, and some are quite accomplished at it. The idea of a beautiful melody, though, is lost on most of them.

For deaf people, translated songs are close to the kind of poetry that hearing people call, "traditional." That is, it has a set number of beats in each line, and there is a definite rhyme scheme. When a deaf person watches someone perform a song, it is to him a poem. The signing is more dramatic, more visual, more theatrical, and it is done in rhythmical style. The fact that there is also music is inconsequential to the enjoyment of the piece.

Translating songs into Ameslan has become a popular pastime for many hearing signers and a few deaf people. It presents some rather tricky problems, though, which is why a song is presented in this lesson. First of all, there is no standard translation of any song, even "The Star Spangled Banner." One will see any given song signed in as many ways as there are signers who do it. A popular song from Germany, France, or Russia will usually be rendered in English in such as way as to become the standard way to sing that song in English. Such is not the case in Ameslan. Every translation becomes a new signed version. Even old standbys such as Christmas carols vary from signer to signer. This may seem gloomy, but actually it is not. Each signer may be as creative as he likes, not having to worry about how someone else has signed it. It is interesting to see many versions, rather than only one.

Another problem one is faced with in translating songs is the music itself. One is limited as to how many signs one may use, so that the signing begins and ends with the music. Often this will force one out of straight Ameslan into a pidgin signed English.

When songs are translated from one spoken language to another, a completely new song usually arises from the process. The target language simply may not have the words to express the same ideas as the language of origin, and at the same time keep within the beat of the music. Or, there may be such cultural differences that the original makes little sense in the target language.

If, for example, one translates "jingle bells" into French literally, one gets "les grelots tintinabulent," containing six syllables. The English words have only three syllables. Anyone who can fit "les grelots tintinabulent" to the music of "Jingle Bells" gets my vote! Instead, the French sing, "Vive le vent! Vive le vent!" which means, "Long live the wind!" It has little to do with jingling bells, but it fits the music nicely, and has a snowy feeling about it.

The point of all this is that translators of songs do not feel bound by words. They go for ideas, feelings, moods, imagery, etc. That much latitude, however, has not been taken by most translators of songs into Ameslan. Most of us have felt that we ought to remain pretty well within the ball park as far as matching words with signs is concerned. As a consequence, most of our translations do not make good sense to deaf people, and furthermore the songs come out looking rather stilted. Now, having said all this, let's see how "The Star Spangled Banner" becomes STAR SPECKLE FLAG.

SUNRISE-R LIGHT-RAYS-RD-U FLAG-U//

QM BH:THERE SEE-U CAN#

PAST NIGHT DURING SUNSET-L LIGHT-RAYS(reverse the movement, i.e., close the fingers

as BH move from the "flag" to the "sunset") FLAG WE PRIDE PRAISE#

ALL-NIGHT WAR AWFUL//

WALL STRUCTURE(hold L arm in place) WE LOOK-U(over the L arm)//

"stripes" STAR(L of "stripes") BH:SHINY(from "star")//

BRAVE STILL FLAG(gently waving)#

ROCKET "LH breaks away and signs RED as RH continues upward; then LH joins RH and

both sign a wriggling LIGHT-RAYS softly floating downward"//

LH:CANNON RH:CANNON EXPLOSION-LU EXPLOSION-RU// BH:THERE-U SEE-U

CAN STILL FLAG(gently waving)# QM THAT-U STAR-UL SPECKLE-UL "stripes-UR"

NOW DAY CONTINUE FLAG(gently waving)//

IN COUNTRY FOR PEOPLE BH:THERE FREE//

AND HOME FOR PEOPLE BRAVE#

VOCABULARY AND TRANSLATION NOTES

A flag, a banner; a flag waving in the breeze.

FLAG

To sing; song, music. Since music for most deaf people is of little consequence, this one sign covers such terms as **"melody," "harmony," "ballad,"** etc.

MUSIC

To quote; quotation marks, a quotation. This sign is often used to indicate the title of something, in which case it is glossed by **the title,** or **entitled.**

QUOTE

To excerpt, to quote something from printed matter, to extract from a book or newspaper. Some idiomatic uses of QUOTE are discussed at the end of this lesson.

EXCERPT

To speckle, to dot; speckled, dotted. If this sign is done on the face it might mean **freckles,** or **measles.**

SPECKLE

A star

STAR

MUSIC QUOTE STAR SPECKLE FLAG "The Star Spangled Banner"

The signs MUSIC QUOTE are usually used to inform the audience that you are about to do a song called . . . (whatever the title is).

One would hope that before anyone attempted to translate a word like "spangled," one would be sure to know its meaning. According to the dictionary the word refers to bright shiny objects, such as pieces of metal, or things like sequins. Why then do I sign SPECKLE instead of SHINY? Because that is the way it is usually signed in this song. I admit that the answer is not very noble, but one sometimes is wiser to go with tradition. At any rate, the SPECKLE sign says that the flag is dotted with stars, and that is a fact.

Rays of light. The wriggling of the fingers, the movement of the hands, and the direction of movement all determine what kind of light it is, its brightness, and what its source is.

LIGHT-RAYS

There, at that place, over there. This sign appears mainly in songs, poems, prayers, and theatrical signing. Usually "there" is shown simply by indexing. Often in these elevated prose statements, the sign might mean, **you,** and would be comparable to the English, **thou,** or **thee.**

THERE

Question mark. This is a cue sign which tells W that S is about to ask a question. It does not come at the beginning of every question. Such questions as, "How are you?" "Where are you going?" and "What time is it?" would not take the QM sign. This sign is reserved for questions that S feels are of more than everyday significance.

The QM sign is actually a variation of the QUERY sign, and like that sign it can be translated as, "Do you . . . ?" "Can you . . . ?" etc. Sometimes it comes both at the beginning and at the end of the question.

QM

SUNRISE-R LIGHT-RAYS-RD-U FLAG-U// QM BH:THERE $\overline{\text{SEE-U CAN}}$# "Oh say can you see, by the dawn's early light."

A transliteration of the Ameslan here is: "The sun rises; the light rays shine from the sun upwards to the flag. Can you see it?" This order of signs reflects the pattern of setting the scene, then describing it, referring to it, reacting to it, or asking about it.

Here QM is used to cue the audience that an important (or in this case, a dramatic) question is about to be asked.

The THERE sign should refer to the audience, thus meaning "all of you."

The SEE sign moves upward toward the "flag."

Be sure to have a questioning expression as you sign SEE-U CAN.

If the music is slow enough, you may add another QM at the end, after CAN.

To be proud; pride.

PRIDE

**To praise, to applaud; to congratulate;
congratulations, Bravo!**

PRAISE

PAST NIGHT DURING SUNSET-L LIGHT-RAYS(reverse the movement, i.e., close the fingers as BH move from the "flag" to the "sunset") FLAG WE PRIDE PRAISE# "What so proudly we hailed at the twilight's last gleaming?"

The transliteration goes: "Last night, as the sun was setting, the light faded from the flag toward the sun; the flag we proudly praised."

If you think of the DURING sign as meaning, "while" and "as" then it will come naturally to you to use it to gloss for the English "when" and "at," in statements like the one above.

The reversal of the finger movements in the LIGHT-RAYS sign is purely an aesthetic variation that visualizes the fading sunlight.

Bar, "stripes." The reason for the quotation marks here is that this gesture is more a mimetic representation than a sign. It can mean whatever is being discussed at the moment. It might be a cartoon strip, or the shape of a window. If placed against the body, it could mean stripes of colors on a dress. It could be a bar or rail, or a newspaper headline.

BAR; "STRIPES"

To shine, to glitter; shiny, glittery. If the shiny object has been spatialized, then the sign moves from the object. For example, to say that someone has shiny, sparkling eyes, both hands would begin near S's eyes and move outwards.

SHINY

(1) To be brave, to be courageous; to be confident; brave, bravery, courage; confidence; (2) to be well, to be healthy; health, strength, wellbeing.

BRAVE

Over, above. When OVER is done with a large sweep of the arm, it means **all over, over a large area.**

When OVER is combined with DIRT (DIRT OVER) it means a large expanse of land, a nation, countryside, etc.

OVER

A structure, a building. This is a rather new sign and might be understood by many deaf people as simply piling something on top of something else.

STRUCTURE

A wall, a fence, an enclosure. Sometimes the palms are turned outward.

WALL

To war; a war, a battle. Often this sign is used figuratively to indicate **a great struggle.**

WAR

ALL-NIGHT WAR AWFUL//
WALL STRUCTURE(hold L arm in place) WE LOOK-U(over the L arm)//
"stripes" STAR(L of "stripes") BH:SHINY(from "stars")//
BRAVE STILL FLAG(gently waving)#

"Whose broad stripes and bright stars,
Through the perilous fight,
O'er the ramparts we watched,
Were so gallantly streaming."

Before attempting to translate these four lines, one must first change their order so that the time sequence is exact.

Through the perilous fight,
O'er the ramparts we watched,
The broad stripes and bright stars,
Still gallantly streaming.

The new arrangement of lines follows the Ameslan pattern of stating first the time element, then the place, and finally what happened there. The stars and stripes are next established because they are the concrete things; then they are shown to be waving in the breeze.

We are lucky here that the last line of the English (Were so gallantly streaming), and the last line of the Ameslan (BRAVE STILL FLAG) coincide, so that we see the flag "streaming" as we hear the word. It does not always work out this nicely.

By rearranging the English lines, we eliminate the word, "whose," which could not have been translated easily.

The word, "o'er" does not need to be translated (OVER) since the LOOK-U sign moving over the left arm shows the action. Never sign it when you can show it!

Cannon, artillery, a big gun.

CANNON

**An explosion, a loud burst of noise, a
bomb going off,** etc.

EXPLOSION

A rocket, a missile.

ROCKET

ROCKET "LH breaks away and signs RED as RH continues upward; then LH joins RH and both sign a wriggling LIGHT-RAYS softly floating downward"//
LH:CANNON RH:CANNON EXPLOSION-LU EXPLOSION-RU// BH:THERE-U SEE-U CAN STILL FLAG (gently waving)#

"And the rockets' red glare,
The bombs bursting in air,
Gave proof through the night,
That our flag was still there."

Ordinarily STILL would follow FLAG, but it is not as interesting a sign, and it is more difficult to sustain it until the music ends. The FLAG sign can be sustained indefinitely, thus giving S a visually interesting way to mark time until the next line begins.

No attempt is made to translate "through the night" because it has been established earlier, and there has been no time change.

QM THAT-U STAR-UL SPECKLE-UL "stripes-UR" NOW DAY CONTINUE $\overline{\text{FLAG}}$(gently
$\overline{\text{waving)}}$//
IN COUNTRY FOR PEOPLE BH:THERE FREE//
AND HOME FOR PEOPLE BRAVE#

"Oh say does that star spangled banner yet wave,
O'er the land of the free,
And the home of the brave?"

One could use the OVER sign here, but I prefer to be a bit more concrete and say, "in the country," rather than "over the land."

There is no sign for "of," so I use here the sign FOR, to express the idea of a country for free and brave people.

The sign FREE by itself does not convey the idea of "free people" very well, so I became more literal and sign PEOPLE.

The THERE sign here means more literally, "you people out there."

The NOW DAY sign brings the time more concretely up to the immediate present.

If one wanted to go all out for a straight Ameslan version of "The Star Spangled Banner," one would first have to rearrange the thoughts so that they follow the time-sequence principle, and the concrete-first principle, in short, an arrangement that appeals to the eye rather than the ear. It might look something like this:

At twilight's last gleaming,
While the terrible war raged on,
From the ramparts we watched
The stars and stripes waving in the wind.

With great pride we cheered!
All through the night
The rockets burst, and the bombs exploded,
And we could see that the flag was still there.
When the sun rose the next day,
We asked, "Is the flag still there?"
Today we ask, "Does that flag wave still,"
In the land of free people,
And the home of brave people?"

The next step would be to find the best signs to convey these thoughts and images, and that would keep within the timing of the music. I leave that to those who are interested in pursuing it further.

IDIOM WORK

In addition to its other meanings, the QUOTE sign may be used to convey the feeling that the sign preceding it is not to be taken literally. When it is used this way, the QUOTE sign is shaken slightly in a jittery fashion.

INX-R GOOD MAN QUOTE# "He's a good man, so to speak," or "In his way," or "He's nominally good."

The attitude of the signer may be one of good humor, kidding, or sarcasm.

INX-R B-O-S-S QUOTE# "He thinks he's the boss," or "He's the nominal boss," or, "Ostensibly, he's the boss," or "He's kind of like the boss."

A signer might sign, INX-R $\overset{?}{\overline{\text{SICK}}}$#, and the watcher might respond, QUOTE#, which could mean, "Well, sort of sick," "Not really, just kind of."

EXERCISE

Practice signing "The Star Spangled Banner," with music, until you can sign it smoothly and without hesitation.

SIGN NEW MANY

Meat, flesh. There are no signs for specific cuts of meat, such as "steak," "roast," "chop," etc., these are fingerspelled.

MEAT

Enough, plenty, sufficient, ample.

ENOUGH

To fill, to fill up; full, full of, filled up.

FULL

The numeral "one hundred."

100 (ONE HUNDRED)

A dollar, a dollar bill; dollars.

DOLLAR

Maximum; up to (a point). This sign is used when S wishes to set a limit on the number of things being discussed.

MAXIMUM

An apple, apples.

APPLE

To limit, to restrict; limit, limitation.

LIMIT

The numeral "five."

5 (FIVE)

The numeral "three."

3 (THREE)

More than, in excess of, over.

MORE-THAN

One movement: **a month.** Two movements:
months, monthly.

MONTH

Less than, under.

LESS-THAN

To be divorced, to get divorced; divorce.

DIVORCE

1. MONEY FOR MEAT $\overline{\text{ENOUGH HAVE}}^{?}$#
   "Is there enough money for (some) meat?"
   "Do we have enough money for (the) meat?"

2. CAR FULL MORE CAN'T#
   "My car's full I can't take any more."

3. EARN 100 DOLLAR MAXIMUM FINISH#
   "You can only earn up to a hundred dollars."

4. APPLE LIMIT 5#
   "You can only have five apples."
   "You are limited to five apples."

5. THEY-2 MARRY 3 YEAR MORE-THAN#
   "They've been married over (more than) three years."

6. THEY-2 MARRY 1 MONTH LESS-THAN// DIVORCE#
   "They were married less than a month when they got divorced."
   "They hadn't been married a month when they were divorced."

Last year, a year ago.

LAST-YEAR

To increase, to get larger.

INCREASE

The numeral "twenty."

20 (TWENTY)

Annually, year after year, every year, yearly.

ANNUALLY

Next year.

NEXT-YEAR

Bicycle.

BICYCLE

New; news.

NEW

7. LAST-YEAR INCREASE 20 L-B ME#
     "I put on (gained) twenty pounds last year."

    There is no sign for "pound," it is usually spelled L-B, or L-B-S.

8. COST INCREASE-U^2 ANNUALLY#
     "Costs (Taxes) keep going up every year."
     As you repeat INCREASE be sure to move it upward. By reversing the INCREASE sign and moving it downward, you get the idea of something decreasing in size over a period of time.

9. NEXT-YEAR BICYCLE NEW BUY ME#
     "I'm gonna buy a new bike next year."

The numeral "four."

4 (FOUR)

To add; addition.

ADD

The numeral "six."

6 (SIX)

The numeral "seven."

7 (SEVEN)

To subtract, to take away; subtraction.

SUBTRACT

**To leave a thing, to be left; residue, re-
mainder.**

LEAVE

The numeral "eight."

8 (EIGHT)

The numeral "nine."

9 (NINE)

The numeral "ten." When 10 combines with another number, you have a "teen," 10⌢3, 10⌢4, 10⌢5, etc. (thirteen, fourteen, fifteen, etc.).

10 (TEN)

To get worse; to multiply; to figure, to reckon; multiplication; arithmetic.

WORSE

To divide, to split.

DIVIDE

10. 4≡LH:2(under RH) ADD 6#
    "Four and two are (make) six."

When giving two numbers to be added, place one above the other. An alternative is to make the numbers with BH simultaneously side by side, then the ADD sign moves horizontally, not vertically and looks like MEETING.

11. 7≡LH:3(under RH) SUBTRACT (LEAVE) 4#
    "Three from seven is (leaves) four."
    "Seven take away three is four."

This sentence may be signed: 7 SUBTRACT 3 LEAVE 4#

12. SCHOOL ESTABLISH YEAR 18 17#
    "The school was founded in 1817."

13. 2≡LH:9 WORSE 18#
    "Two nines are eighteen."
    "Two times nine is eighteen."

14. 10≡LH:5 DIVIDE 2#
    "Ten divided by five is two."
    "Five goes into ten two times."

Cosmetic make up.

MAKE-UP

To remove, to take away, to take down, to take out.

REMOVE

A picture, a photograph, a painting. When reference is made to a picture in a book, the LH will usually be held with the palm up, and the bottom of the RH will rest on the palm of the LH.

PICTURE

Ugly, ugliness. This may refer to physical ugliness, and to behavior being ugly.

UGLY

A hat, a cap, anything that is on top of the head; the top of the head.

HAT

To take one's hat off, to remove one's hat.

HAT-OFF

CANDY

Candy. This sign varies around the country, check it out with local deaf people.

SHARE

To share, to divide up. When SHARE is moved around in a circle, it would imply **to share among everyone.** When it is used with money, it means, **change.**

To go together; to pool; roommate, partner.

ROOMMATE

15. MAKE-UP NOT⌢NEED REMOVE#
    "Take that make up off, you don't need it."

Normally the NOT would follow that which it negates, but NOT⌢NEED is the way these two signs usually appear. This sentence could also be signed, MAKE-UP REMOVE NOT⌢NEED#.

16. PICTURE UGLY BH:REMOVE#
    "Take that picture down, it's ugly."
    "Take that ugly picture down."

17. (HAT) HAT-OFF#
    "Take your hat off."

18. CANDY SHARE(move in circle)#
    "Share the candy with the rest of us."

To separate, to part; separation.

SEPARATE

Toilet, restroom, bathroom.

TOILET

To use up, to consume, to be all out of.

USED-UP

One dollar, a dollar bill; first.

1-DOLLAR; FIRST

To get used to, to be in the habit of; habit, used to something.

HABIT

To change, to modify, to adapt, to convert.

CHANGE

To be hard like a rock; rock.

HARD

To be difficult, to be hard. This sign rarely refers to a hard object.

HARD

A horse, horses.

HORSE

To count, to enumerate.

COUNT

To be foolish; fool.

FOOL

19. LONG-AGO THEY-2 ROOMMATE// NOW SEPARATE#
"They used to be roommates, but now they've parted."

20. TOILET PAPER USED-UP#
"There's no more toilet paper."
"The toilet paper's all gone."
"The toilet paper's used up."

21. 1-DOLLAR $\overline{\text{SHARE (HAVE) YOU}}^{?}$#
"Do you have change for a dollar?"
"Can you change a dollar?"

22. HABIT OLD CHANGE HARD#
"Old habits are hard to change."

23. HORSE COUNT $\overline{\text{FINISH YOU}}^{?}$#
"Did you count the horses?"
"Have you counted the horses?"

24. $\overline{\text{FOOL YOU}}^{!}$#
"You're a fool!"
"You fool, you!"

To be silly; silly.

SILLY

To carry on, to fool around, to horse around, to clown, to be ridiculous.

SILLY-FOOLING

To waste, to be wasteful.

WASTE

To be skillful, to be skilled, to be adept, to be proficient, to be good at; skill, expert, talent.

SKILL

To be equal; equals.

EQUAL

To be even, to be equal, to be level; even, level.

EVEN

To vary, to fluctuate, to vacillate.

VARY

To complain, to gripe, to groan, to grumble; to protest, to object.

COMPLAIN

To notify, to inform, to tell, to report, to let someone know, to announce.

NOTIFY

To obey, to be obedient. The NOTIFY and the OBEY signs are rarely signed as they are shown here. Both of them are usually signed alike, that is, with the LH somewhere between the chest and the face, and out from the body as shown in the following photo.

OBEY

NOTIFY; OBEY

A shoe; a pair of shoes.

SHOE

Small.

SMALL

Bad.

BAD

Ignorant, uninformed, uneducated.

IGNORANT

Dumb, stupid, thickheaded.

DUMB

25. SILLY FINISH#
"Stop being silly!"
"Don't be silly!"

26. SILLY-FOOLING WASTE TIME#
"That horsing around wastes time."

27. SKILL EQUAL(move in circle) NOT// VARY#
"We are not equal in ability, we vary."

28. BH:COMPLAIN NOTIFY-ME DON'T#
"Don't tell me your complaints." *(NOTIFY-ME means to move NOTIFY out then back to S.)*

29. SHOE SMALL#
"My shoes are too small."

30. NOTIFY BAD MUST// SORRY#
"I regret that I have to tell you some bad news."
"I've got some bad news for you, sorry."

31. IGNORANT ME MAYBE// DUMB NOT#
"I may be ignorant, but I'm not dumb."

A light bulb, a light, an electric light.

LIGHT-BULB

To invent, to create, to make up.

INVENT

The letter "I."

I

Fantastic, beyond belief, incredible, unbelievable. Usually with a negative feeling.

FANTASTIC

To break; broken.

BREAK

To turn out/off the lights; the lights are out/off. The way the sign is shown here it refers to overhead lights. If the "lights" face forward, then it might refer to automobile headlights.

LIGHTS-OFF

To turn on the lights; the lights are on. Like the LIGHTS-OFF sign, the direction the hands face implies different types of lights.

LIGHTS-ON

32. LIGHT-BULB INVENT WHO// E-D-I-S-O-N#
"Edison invented the light-bulb." (Notice that this is a rhetorical question.)
"It was Edison who invented the light bulb."

33. STORY FANTASTIC YOU#
"That tale of yours is pure fantasy."
"You talk crazy."

34. LIGHT-BULB BREAK#
"The light's broken."

35. LIGHTS-OFF WHY#
"Why are lights out?"
"Why'd the lights go out?"

36. LIGHTS-ON PLEASE#
"Turn on the lights, please."

37. LIGHTS-ON LIGHTS-OFF $\overline{FOR^2}$#
"What are you flashing the lights for?"

The two signs, LIGHTS-ON and LIGHTS-OFF, would actually be repeated two or three times rapidly, without moving the hands up or down.

When FOR is repeated with a questioning expression, it means, "why," "what for," "how come," etc.

To fly in an airplane; an airplane. The AIRPLANE sign is very directional. When S wants to indicate "an airplane," he will usually make the sign with a repeated slight movement.

AIRPLANE

New York, New York City.

NEW-YORK

Any.

ANY

A wedding.

WEDDING

Formal, proper; courteous, well mannered.

FORMAL

To con, to victimize, to gull, to swindle, to take advantage of someone. Usually with a negative feeling.

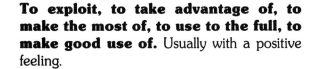

CON

To exploit, to take advantage of, to make the most of, to use to the full, to make good use of. Usually with a positive feeling.

EXPLOIT

To go on vacation; to be free, to have free time, to have leisure time; vacation, holiday.

VACATION

To be angry, to get angry.

ANGRY

To forget.

FORGET

38. NEW-YORK AIRPLANE-R-S ME#
"I flew in from New York."

39. COME-HERE-W-S ANY TIME YOU#
"Come see me anytime."

40. WEDDING LARGE FORMAL $\overline{\text{WANT YOU}}^?$#
"Do you want a big, formal wedding?"

41. CON SKILL INX-R#
"He's a real con artist."
"He's clever at taking people in."

42. NOW $\overline{\text{VACATION}}^{\text{if}}$// STUDY EXPLOIT#
"If you've got some free time use it to study."
"Take advantage of your vacation, study."

To pay, to pay off.

PAY

To be cross, to be irate, to be vexed, to be peeved; annoyed, huffy, pouting; bad mood.

CROSS

To disgust, to repel, to turn one's stom-ach, to nauseate; to have an upset stomach.

DISGUST

Numskull, idiot, pea-brain, blockhead, dolt.

NUMSKULL

**To associate with, to relate to, to inter-
act with, to have fellowship with, to mix
with; each other.**

ASSOCIATE

43. ME ANGRY WHY// FORGET PAY-W-S YOU#
"I'm angry (mad) because you forgot to pay me." (Another rhetorical question.)

44. CROSS ALL-DAY YOU// WHY#
"You've been in a bad mood (cross) all day, why?"

45. SILLY-FOOLING INX-R DISGUST#
"His cutting up turns my stomach."

46. MEAT OLD DISGUST#
"The meat was old, it made me sick.#

47. CAR NEW $\overline{\text{BUY YOU}}^?$// $\overline{\text{NUMSKULL YOU}}^!$#
"You bought a new car? You idiot!"

48. SIGN SKILL BECOME $\overset{\text{if}}{\overline{\text{WANT}}}$// DEAF ASSOCIATE MUST YOU#
"If you want to be (become) a skilled signer, you must associate with deaf people."

To be born; birth.

BORN

A problem. The idea of "problem" may also be conveyed with the DIFFICULT sign, or the WORRY sign.

PROBLEM

To beckon, to summon, to call.

BECKON

To beckon me, to summon me, to call me.

BECKON-ME

To appear, to become visible, to show
up, to turn up, to arise, to pop up.

APPEAR

To ignore, to take no notice of; to ne-
glect, to disregard, to not take care of.

IGNORE

To criticize; to grade, to correct.

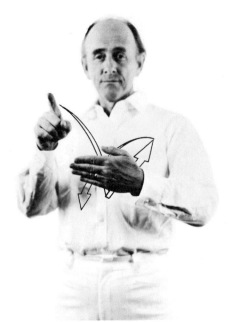

CRITICIZE

49. $\overline{\text{NOW BORN DAY}}^{?}$// OLD HOW-MANY YOU#
    "Today's your birthday, how old are you?" (There are a number of signs for "birthday." Check with the deaf people in your area.)

50. $\overline{\text{READY}}^{if}$// BECKON-ME#
    "Call me when you're ready."

51. PROBLEM MELT MUST YOU#
    "You must solve the problem."
    "You've got to resolve the difficulty."

52. PROBLEM $\overline{\text{APPEAR}}^{if}$// IGNORE CAN'T#
    "If a problem comes up, you can't ignore it."

53. TEST CRITICIZE $\overline{\text{FINISH}}^{?}$#
    "Have you graded (corrected) the tests?"

To be hungry, to hunger; to wish for, to desire; to be filled with passion, to lust.

HUNGRY

To hide, to conceal.

HIDE

To search for, to look for, to hunt for.

SEARCH

To defeat, to beat, to conquer, to overcome.

DEFEAT

To put, to place.

PUT

To move. This sign relates to physically moving something from one place to another.

MOVE

To move, to be in motion. This sign generally refers to a person moving himself, or to moving a thing back and forth. Think of the meaning as the opposite of "being still."

MOVEMENT

To freeze; to be absolutely still; to be at a standstill; to be arrested or cut short in growth; ice.

FREEZE

To be young; youth.

YOUNG

To be brilliant; bright, clever, witty.

CLEVER

The police, cops.

POLICE

54. TIME EAT PASS// HUNGRY ME#
"It's past dinner time and I'm hungry."

55. DRESS NEW HAVE HUNGRY#
"I wish I had (some) new clothes (a new dress)."

56. SHOE HIDE INX-R// SEARCH FIND CAN'T ME#
"He hid my shoes. I've looked all over and I can't find them."

57. DEFEAT-R-S DEFEAT-S-R EQUAL-R#
"They beat us, we beat them, we're even."

58. SIT MOVE-L-R PLEASE#
"Please move your chair (desk)."

59. MOVEMENT DON'T// FREEZE#
"Don't move, keep absolutely still."

60. LONG-AGO YOUNG ME// CLEVER// NOW OLD// IGNORANT#
"When I was young I knew it all, now that I'm old, I don't know anything."

To scare, to be scared, to be afraid.

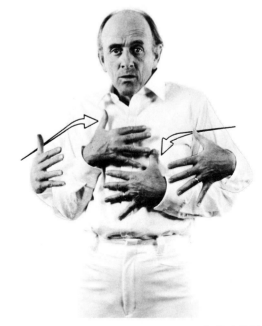

SCARE

To flee, to run away, to escape, to split.

FLEE

To fear, to be afraid; to be in awe of. The SCARE sign denotes a more common everyday kind of fear. The FEAR sign is more the kind of fear one has of the unknown, a generalized kind of fear that may not have a recognizable cause.

FEAR

To be sad, to grieve; sadness, grief.

SAD

To be secretive; to keep a secret; secret.

SECRET

61. POLICE SEE-R// SCARE FLEE-L YOU#
    "When you saw the police, you got scared and took off."

Notice that the FLEE sign goes to the opposite side of the SL from where the police are supposed to be.

62. FEAR-L-S² INX-R// SAD TRUE#
    "He's afraid of everything (his own shadow), it's really sad."

If "he" is right of the SL, then the FEAR sign is made as if to show that the cause of the fear comes from the left of the SL.

63. NOTIFY SAD#
    "I've got some sad news for you."

64. SECRET TATTLE EASY YOU#
    "You can't keep a secret."
    "You tell secrets too easily."

To show, to display, to exhibit.

SHOW

To take up; to assume the role of. This sign implies that S is acquiring some new behavior, or information. It is the sign to use, for example, if S wishes to say, "I'm taking a course in Spanish," or "I took up golf last week." It is also used in such expressions as, "I'll play the role of Hamlet."

TAKE-UP

To interpret, to translate.

INTERPRET

The world.

WORLD

To travel.

TRAVEL

To be lazy, to loaf; lazy.

LAZY

Very, exceedingly, so.

VERY

65. MONEY LOSE WHERE// SHOW-W-S#
    "Show me where you lost the money."

66. LAST-YEAR FRANCE $\overline{\text{TAKE-UP YOU}}^?$#
    "Did you take French last year?"

67. SOME THING BUY MUST ME#
    "I need to buy some things."

68. ONLY THING BUY MUST ME#
    "I need to buy something."

69. INTERPRET SKILL GOAL ME#
    "I want to be a skilled interpreter."

70. WORLD TRAVEL FINISH INX-R#
    "He's been (traveled) all over the world."

71. LAZY $\overline{\text{VERY}}^!$ INX-R#
    "He's very lazy!"
    "He is so lazy!"

To improve, to get better. If the motion of the RH is a sweeping one, rather than the type shown in the picture, it conveys the idea that the improvement is in progress, i.e. **improving, getting better; refurbishing, renovating,** etc.

IMPROVE

To join, to become a member of; to be related to, to be relevant to; to belong to; to unite, to connect.

JOIN

To be careful, to take care, to be cautious.

CAREFUL

To be dark, to become dark; dark, darkness; night.

DARK

To have a pain or ache, to hurt.

PAIN

HURT

To hurt, to be hurt, to be in pain. The PAIN and HURT signs are very similar in meaning. The PAIN sign may be a bit more acute and intense than the HURT sign. Both signs may be placed on various parts of the body to indicate where the pain is, for example if they are put on the forehead, it would mean "headache."

One movement: **to injure, to harm; to per-secute, to torture; to tease.** Several soft movements: **to tease.**

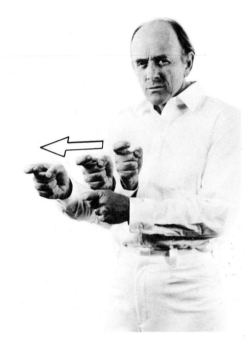

INJURE

To supervise, to look after, to take care of, to watch over, to guard.

SUPERVISE

To vote, to elect; vote, election.

VOTE

An institution; a residential school for deaf children.

INSTITUTION

Short; shortly. This sign, like its opposite LONG, usually refers to length of time.

SHORT

72. SIGN IMPROVE YOU#
   "Your signing has improved."
   "Your signing is improving (sweeping motion of the RH)."

73. C-L-U-B JOIN $\overline{\text{FINISH}}^?$ YOU#
   "Did you join the club?"

74. CAREFUL HURT WILL#
   "Be careful, you'll get hurt."

75. DARK $\overset{\text{if}}{\overline{\text{READ}}}$ EYES INJURE WILL# *(Point to your eyes for EYES.)*
   "If you read in poor light you'll ruin your eyes."

76. MONEY SUPERVISE AGENT $\overset{\text{if}}{\overline{\text{VOTE}}}// \overline{\text{ACCEPT}}^? YOU#$
   "If you're elected treasurer, will you accept?"

   The first three signs denote the person who takes care of the money, the treasurer.

77. ME SUPERVISE INSTITUTION INX-R#
   "I'm a dorm counselor in the school for deaf children."

To be relieved, to heave a sigh of relief.

RELIEF

To be satisfied, to satisfy; satisfaction.

SATISFY

Way, path, street, road; manner, method, technique.

WAY

A flower.

FLOWER

Autumn, Fall; in the Autumn/Fall.

AUTUMN

Pretty, lovely, beautiful, attractive.

PRETTY

To lie, to tell a lie; a lie.

LIE

To depend on, to rely upon.

DEPEND

To be responsible; responsibility; burden; fault.

RESPONSIBLE

78. MOVIE SHORT// SATISFY NOT#
    "The movie is short, it leaves me unsatisfied."

79. LIVE WAY NAME E-L-M INX-R#
    "I live on Elm Street."

80. DURING SUMMER FLOWER GROW MANY#
    "Many flowers grow in the summer."

81. DURING AUTUMN TREE-L-R PRETTY#
    "In autumn the trees (the woods) are beautiful."

82. LIE³ INX-R// DEPEND-R DON'T#
    "Don't depend on him, he lies all the time."
    "You can't take his word, he's always lying."

83. CONTROL RESPONSIBLE WHO#
    "Who's responsible for running this?"
    "Who's in charge?"

Family.

FAMILY

To be poor; poverty.

POOR

To pity, to have pity on, to be merciful, to feel sorry for, to sympathize with. This sign is often used sarcastically to say, "Oh, you poor thing," or "Poor baby!"

PITY

Pants, trousers, a pair of pants.

PANTS

A shirt, a blouse.

SHIRT

To be dirty; dirty, filthy, messy.

DIRTY

Hair.

HAIR

The color yellow. When used with hair it means blond.

YELLOW

False, not true, fake, phony; artificial.

FALSE

To dye; dye.

DYE

To copy, to make a copy; to imitate.

COPY

To punish.

PUNISH

College.

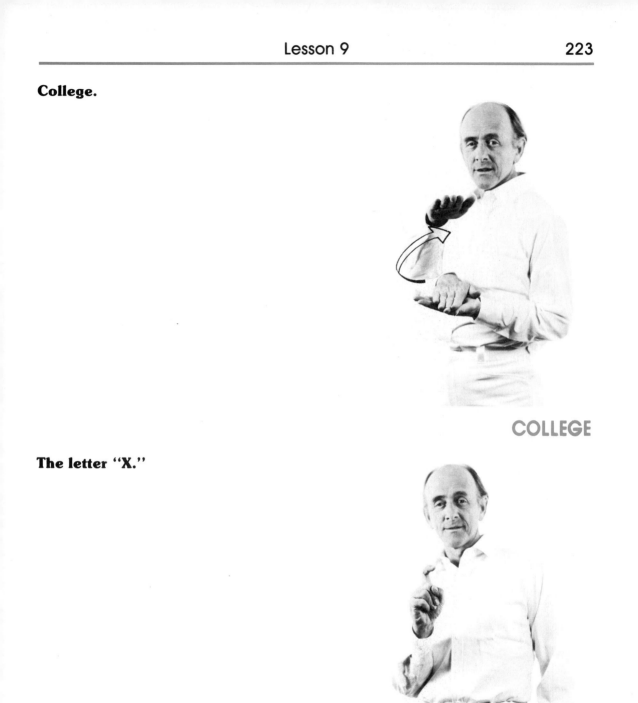

COLLEGE

The letter "X."

X

A word, words.

WORD

From, whence.

FROM

Rome, Roman, Latin.

ROME

84. ITS-R FAMILY POOR BUT// BH:PITY-R DON'T-WANT INX-R#
"His family's poor, but they don't want pity."

85. PANTS SHIRT DIRTY YOU// HOW#
"How'd your pants and shirt get so dirty?"

86. HAIR YELLOW FALSE// DYE INX-R#
"His hair isn't really blond, he dyed it."

87. TEST COPY-L YOU// PUNISH WILL ME#
"If you copy on the test I'll punish you."

88. COLLEGE E-X 55 ME#
"I was in the class of '55, but I didn't graduate."

This expression is the type used by deaf people who attended Gallaudet College, but did not graduate. They refer to themselves as "ex's."

89. ENGLAND WORD FROM ROME MANY#
"A lot of English words come from Latin."

To be careless; careless, reckless.

CARELESS

To notice, to take notice of, to spot, to see out of the corner of your eye.

NOTICE

To be smart. Not quite as smart as CLEVER.

SMART

To be smart, to know a lot; studious, scholarly. This too is smarter than SMART. It differs from CLEVER in that it refers to knowing a great deal, as opposed to being bright or clever.

SCHOLARLY

To be conceited; big-headed.

CONCEIT

To burn; fire.

FIRE

To hurry, to rush.

HURRY

Cigaret.

CIGARET

Cigaret or cigar smoking.

SMOKING

A pipe.

PIPE

Nerve, gall, cheek, crust, chutzpah.

NERVY

90. CLEVER INX-R BUT// CARELESS#
"He's bright, but he's careless."

91. SMART BUT SCHOLARLY NOT INX-R#
"He's smart, but he's no scholar."

92. UP-TIL-NOW NOTICE CONCEIT INCREASE-U² YOU#
"I've noticed lately that you've been getting more and more conceited."

93. NOW MORNING FIRE PRACTICE HAVE WILL#
"There will be a fire drill this morning."

94. DURING PRACTICE// RAPID-RUN HURRY DON'T// LINE-UP-R-L SLOW QUIET#
"Don't run or hurry, walk in a line, slowly and quietly during the drill."

95. CIGARET SMOKING ILLEGAL// PIPE ALLRIGHT#
"You can't smoke cigarets, but pipes are okay."

96. QUERY-R-S LEND-R 10 DOLLAR// $\overline{\text{NERVE}}$ INX-R#
"The nerve of that guy! He asked me to lend him ten dollars!"

Bread, a slice of bread, a loaf of bread.

BREAD

Butter; margarine.

BUTTER

To condense, to abbreviate, to be brief, to be concise; to take a short cut.

CONDENSE

Mail; letter.

MAIL

A lesson; a message.

LESSON

97. BREAD WITH BUTTER $\overline{\text{WANT}}^?$#
   "Do you want butter with the bread?"

98. STORY LONG CONDENSE PLEASE#
   "Your story's too long, please condense (shorten) it."

99. MAIL ARRIVE $\overline{\text{FINISH}}^?$#
   "Has the mail arrived yet?"

100. LESSON BH:FINISH// BOOK END#
   "The lesson's done, this is the end of the book."

INDEX